# HOUSE RULES

## DANCE WITH ME

## ERIC REESE

THE BAD BOY

*For all the house music lovers out there!*

If there's a book that you want to read, but it hasn't been written yet, then you must write it.

TONI MORRISON

# CONTENTS

# CHAPTER ONE

## HOUSE MUSIC

House music is a genre of electronic music created by club DJs and music producers in Chicago in the early 1980s. Early house music was generally characterized by repetitive 4/4 beats, rhythms mainly provided by drum machines, off-beat hi-hat cymbals, and synthesized basslines. While house displayed several characteristics similar to disco music, which preceded and influenced it, as both were DJ and record producer-created dance music, house was more electronic and minimalistic. The mechanical, repetitive rhythm of house was more important than the song itself; indeed, many house songs were instrumental, with no vocals, or if there was singing, the singer (typically female) would not be well-known, or there would be no words.

House music developed in Chicago's underground dance

club culture in the early 1980s, as DJs from the gay subculture began altering the pop-like disco dance tracks to give them a more mechanical beat and deeper basslines. As well, these DJs began to mix synth pop, dub reggae, rap and even jazz into their tracks. House tracks were pioneered by Chicago DJ/record producer Frankie Knuckles, the Chicago acid-house electronic music group Phuture, the Tennessee DJ/producer Mr. Fingers, and US-born, UK-based singer Kym Mazelle and was associated with African-American and gay subcultures. House music quickly spread to other American cities such as Detroit, New York City, Baltimore, and Newark – all of which developed their own regional scenes. In the mid-to-late 1980s, house music became popular in Europe as well as major cities in South America, and Australia.

Early house music had commercial success in Europe, with songs such as "Pump Up The Volume" by MARRS (1987), "Theme from S'Express" by S'Express (1988) and "Doctorin' the House" by Coldcut (1988) climbing the pop charts. Since the early to mid-1990s, house music has been infused into mainstream pop and dance music worldwide. In the late 1980s, many local Chicago house music artists suddenly found themselves presented with major label deals. House music proved to be a commercially successful genre and a more mainstream pop-based variation grew increasingly popular. In the late 1990s to the 2010s, progressive house artists/performers such as Daft Punk, Basement Jaxx, and House of 909 brought new attention to house.

House music since 2010, while keeping several of these core elements, notably the prominent kick drum on every beat, varies widely in style and influence, ranging from the soulful and atmospheric deep house to the more minimalistic microhouse. It has also fused with several other genres creating fusion subgenres, such as euro house, tech house, electro house and jump house. One subgenre, acid house, was based around the squelchy, deep electronic tones created by Roland's TB-303 bassline machine.

Artists and groups such as Madonna, Janet Jackson, Paula Abdul, CeCe Peniston, Bananarama, Robin S., Steps, Kylie Minogue, Björk, and C+C Music Factory all incorporated house into their works in the 1990s and beyond. After enjoying significant success in the early to mid-1990s, house music grew even larger during the second wave of progressive house (1999–2001). The genre has remained popular and fused into other popular subgenres; Ghetto house, deep house and tech house. As of 2016, house music remains popular in both clubs and in the mainstream pop scene while retaining a foothold on underground scenes across the globe.

# CHAPTER TWO

## THE BEGINNING OF HOUSE MUSIC

I t all started in Chicago's Southside in 1977, when a new kind of club opened. This new Chicago club called The Warehouse gave House music its name. Frankie Knuckles, who opened The Warehouse, mixed old disco classics and new Eurobeat pop. It was at this legendary club where many of the experiments were tried. It was also where Acid House got its start.

House was the first direct descendant of disco. In comparison with disco, House was "deeper", "rawer", and more designed to make people dance. Disco had already produced the first records to be aimed specifically at DJs with extended 12" versions that included long percussion breaks for mixing purposes. The early 80s proved a vital turning point. Sinnamon's "Thanks To You", D-Train's "You're The One For Me", and The Peech Boys "Don't

Make Me Wait", a record that has been continually sampled over the last decade, took things in a different direction with their sparse, synthesised sounds that introduced dub effects and drop-outs that had never been heard before.

# CHAPTER THREE

## THE WAREHOUSE

House music did not have its origins just in American music. The popularity of European music, specifically English electronic pop like Depeche Mode and Soft Cell and the earlier, more disco-based sounds of Giorgio Moroder, Klein & MBO, as well as Italian productions, they all gave rise to House music. Two clubs, the already mentioned Chicago's Warehouse and New York's Paradise Garage, which promoted European music, had at the same time broken the barriers of race and sexual preference (for House music was in part targeted at the gay community). Before The Warehouse opened, there had been clubs strictly designed to segregate race. However, The Warehouse did not make any difference between Blacks, Hispanics, or Whites; the main interest was simply music. And the music was as diverse as the clients.

# CHAPTER FOUR

## FRANKIE KNUCKLES

One of the leading DJs at that time was New York born Frankie Knuckles, also called the Godfather of House. Indeed, he was more than a DJ; he was an architect of sound, who experimented with sounds and thus added a new dimension to the art of mixing. In fact, he took the raw material of the disco he spun and added pre-programmed drum tracks to create a constant 4/4 tempo. He played eight to ten hours a night, and the dancers came home exhausted. Thanks to him The Warehouse was regarded as the most atmospheric place in Chicago. The uniqueness of this club lay in a simple mixing of old Philly classics by Harold Melvin, Billy Paul and The O'Jays with disco hits like Martin Circus' "Disco Circus" and imported European pop music by synthesiser groups like Kraftwerk and Telex.

Frankie said, "When we first opened in 1977, I was playing a lot of the East Coast records, the Philly stuff, Salsoul. By '80/81, when that stuff was all over with, I started working a lot of the soul that was coming out. I had to re-construct the records to work for my dancefloor, to keep the dancefloor happy, as there was no dance music coming out! I'd take the existing songs, change the tempo, layer different bits of percussion over them, to make them more conductive for the dancefloor."

# CHAPTER FIVE

## LARRY LEVAN

Frankie's friend, Larry Levan was a black teenager from Brooklyn like Frankie. In fact, it was Larry who first suggested opening The Warehouse in Chicago. However, things took a different turn, and in the end Larry Levan spun in New York's Paradise Garage. Larry Levan and Frankie Knuckles were indeed two very important figures in the development of House music and the modern dance scene. Perhaps there would have been no fame for the two without the producer, DJ and devoted lover of dance and music, David Mancuso, and his dance parties for gays called Loft parties. "The Loft" was a house party intended for a very black and a very gay crowd.

Larry and Frankie attended the Loft parties regularly. It was not only a place of joy but also a place where they became acquainted for the first time with the techniques of House music. Mancuso taught them about creating a perfect House music: about sound, lighting, production, music and DJ techniques.

# CHAPTER SIX

## EIGHTIES PIONEERS OF CHICAGO HOUSE

By the mid 80s, House had emerged in Chicago as a fully developed musical genre through the efforts of Knuckles and those inspired by him like DJ Ron Hardy of Music Box fame. Ron Hardy was another DJ from the gay scene. The sounds they produced differed in that the basis of Knuckle's sound was still disco, whereas Hardy was the DJ that chose the rawest and wildest rhythm tracks he could find.

Besides Frankie Knuckles, Larry Levan, and Ron Hardy, there were other important figures in the development of House music such as Steve "Silk" Hurley, DJ Pierre, Larry Heard, Adonis, Marshall Jefferson and Farley "Jackmaster" Funk, who was a Chicago DJ and producer, as well as a creator of the first international House hit, "Love Can't

Turn Around". DJ Pierre, on the other hand, contributed to the development of Acid House. As a result, a track called "Acid Trax" was produced.

# CHAPTER SEVEN

## THE FOUNDATION OF HOUSE

The term "House music" originated from a Chicago club called The Warehouse, which existed from 1977 to 1983. Clubbers to The Warehouse were primarily black, who came to dance to music played by the club's resident DJ Frankie Knuckles, whom fans refer to as the "godfather of house". Frankie began the trend of splicing together different records when he found that the records he had weren't long enough to satisfy his audience of dancers. He would use tape and a knife to accomplish this. After the Warehouse closed in 1983, the crowds went to Knuckles' new club, The Power Plant.

In the Channel 4 documentary Pump Up The Volume, Knuckles remarks that the first time he heard the term "house music" was upon seeing "we play house music" on a sign in the window of a bar on Chicago's South Side. One of the people in the car with him joked, "you know, that's the kind of music you play down at the Warehouse!", and then everybody laughed. South-Side Chicago DJ Leonard "Remix" Roy, in self-published statements, claims he put such a sign in a tavern window because it was where he played music that one might find in one's home; in his case, it referred to his mother's soul & disco records, which he worked into his sets.

1985 recording "It's House" may also have helped to define this new form of electronic music. However, Chip E. himself lends credence to the Knuckles association, claiming the name came from methods of labeling records at the Importes Etc. record store, where he worked in the early 1980s: bins of music that DJ Knuckles played at the Warehouse nightclub were labelled in the store "As Heard At The Warehouse", which was shortened to simply "House". Patrons later asked for new music for the bins, which Chip E. implies was a demand the shop tried to meet by stocking newer local club hits. In a 1986 interview, when Rocky Jones, the club DJ who ran the D.J. International record label, was asked about the "house" moniker, he did not mention Importes Etc., Frankie Knuckles, or the Warehouse by name. However, he agreed that "house" was a regional catch-all term for dance music, and that it was once synonymous with older disco music, before it became a way to refer to "new" dance music.

Larry Heard, a.k.a. "Mr. Fingers", claims that the term "house" became popular due to many of the early DJs creating music in their own home studios using synthesizers and drum machines, such as the Roland TR-808 programmable drum machine, TR-909, and the TB 303 bassline synth. These synthesizers were used to create a house subgenre called acid house. Juan Atkins, an originator of Detroit techno music, claims the term "house" reflected the exclusive association of particular tracks with particular clubs and DJs; those records helped differentiate the clubs and DJs, and thus were considered to be their "house" records. In an effort to maintain such exclusives, the DJs were inspired to create their own "house" records.

# CHAPTER EIGHT

## THE ORIGINATORS OF HOUSE

There have been various views of who is the inventor of House music. For example, Leonard Remix RRoy asserted that he had given birth to House in May 1981. LRRoy was a remarkable and much respected DJ. He also claimed that he had invented the term "House music" in the spring of 1981.

Chip E. A person who regarded himself as a creator of House music in March of 1985 was Chip E. Yet, there remains a third founder, for he produced "Love Can't Turn Around", one of the biggest selling "House" records. His name is Farley "Jackmaster" Funk. In fact, this big House "cross-over" hit was written, produced and arranged by Jesse Saunders. Jesse, however, did not call himself the creator of House music, but rather used the term "originator", which did not mean that he had invented or created the genre of House music. By "originator" he meant that he "started and/or fused a sound with a lot of different ingredients". Generally speaking, one can say, that there was not just one creator or inventor; on the contrary, House music evolved through the means of collaborative efforts of a few people like Frankie Knuckles, Vince Lawrence, Farley "Jackmaster" Funk, as well as the promoters and labels that made easy the distribution of early House.

The original disco-mixer Walter Gibbons, a white DJ, had a new and immediate impact on the development of Chicago House music. His independent 12" record called "Set It Off" immediately became an underground club anthem. The "Set It Off" sound was primitive House, haunting, repetitive beats ideal for mixing and extending.

# CHAPTER NINE

## THE ROOTS OF HOUSE

House music was created in and by the African American community. Musically, House music evolved in Chicago and New York from African-American musical traditions like gospel, soul, jazz and funk as well as Latin salsa. Spiritually and aesthetically, it developed in the U.S. out of the need of oppressed people, African Americans, gays and Latinos, to build a community through dance , and later in the UK, out of the need of young people dissatisfied with the meaningless materialism of Thatcher's England, to build an alternative community of music and dance via Acid House. From a different point of view, House music in the U.S. was associated with black people, with gay clubs, basically with things that white America would not even acknowledge.

House was just perceived as "gay" music for blacks and thus scorned by whites, although its aim was to unify people of all races, backgrounds and sexual orientations. According to Frankie Knuckles, many people could not and still cannot deal with the fact that House music started in gay clubs. Thus, narrow-mindedness, racism, and even corporate music politics played an important role in preventing House music from flourishing in the U.S. in the eighties.

House music had its origins in gospel, soul and funk rather than in commercial disco music. Furthermore, Chicago jazz, blues and soul had an immense influence on the creation of House music. There were significant Midwestern musical influences that led to the creation of the Chicago flavour of House music. No doubt, the Midwest had its own tradition of African American music. Thus, blues and jazz presented a part of the mix. To sum up, the soul music produced in Chicago, Detroit and Memphis certainly had an impact on Chicago house.

# CHAPTER TEN

## EARLY DJ TECHNIQUES

In the early seventies, the DJs' tools began to improve as the market for dance music began to expand. Yet, the beginnings were hard, for there were only two types of records available, 45s and 33 1/3 LPs, which had "A" sides and "B" sides, and different songs were recorded on both sides. A record which allowed more creativity, namely 12" dance mixes specifically intended for DJs, had not yet appeared on the market. DJs had to manage without basic equipment such as DJ mixers or headphones. What is more, the turntables ran only at two speeds, 45 RPMs and 33 1/3 RPMs. It was impossible to vary the speed, so the turntable moved continuously. In practice, it could be described as follows: DJs started to play one record. Then they took it off the turntable, prepared another record, put this one on and played it. In reality, "putting on and taking off" the record cannot be called mixing. As expected, DJs needed time to change the vinyl disc and thus dancers had to wait between the records.

Turntables There was, however, one way that helped DJs overcome these technical problems. This method was called slip-cueing. The main part of the trick consisted in a duplication of records. In other words, the record collection needed to be copied. DJs had two good turntables at their disposal. They rigged the two tables with a switch into the amplifier so they could move from one to the other. Then they put the same recording on each turntable, to try to extend the mix somehow. The least DJs could do was play the same record twice in pretty rapid succession, which was better than making the dancer wait until they changed the record. Instead of playing the record twice, there was yet another possibility, namely to build the mix by isolating various instrumental, vocal and drum segments and extend them by jumping from record to record.

This technique was probably invented - or at least given currency - by DJ Francis Grosso and widely used by radio station DJs. It required much practice with individual recordings, great agility, and nerves of steel. Great turn-tablists of the seventies like Kool Herc and Grandmaster Flash developed such techniques into an art form.

# CHAPTER ELEVEN

## HOUSE IN THE UK

House music first came to England in the late eighties via the party island of Ibiza. In the summer of 1986, three House records appeared in the top ten: Farley's "Jackmaster" Funk "Love Can't Turn Around", Raze's "Jack The Groove", and Steve "Silk" Hurley's "Jack Your Body". It is said that House music was popularised by the British who invented Acid House and then brought this modified version of House back to the United States. Acid House was perceived differently and that was probably one of the reasons why it attracted the attention of the mainstream. In this way, House music became acceptable dance music also for white folks.

US-born singer Kym Mazelle (born 1960), who moved to the UK, has been called the "First Lady of House Music."

The second best-selling British single of 1988 was an acid house record, the Coldcut-produced "The Only Way Is Up" by Yazz. One of the early club anthems, "Promised Land" by Joe Smooth, was covered and charted within a week by UK band The Style Council. Europeans embraced house, and began booking important American house DJs to play at the big clubs, such as Ministry of Sound, whose resident, Justin Berkmann brought in US pioneer Larry Levan. In the late 1980s, American-born singer Kym Mazelle relocated to London to sign a recording contract with EMI Records and her first album Brilliant! in 1989, which was based on house music. Mazelle's single "Wait!" featuring Robert Howard became an one of the first international house hits.

The house music club scene in cities such as Birmingham, Leeds, Sheffield, Wolverhampton and London were provided with dance tracks by many underground Pirate Radio stations. Club DJs also brought in new house styles, which helped bolster this music genre. The earliest UK house and techno record labels such as Warp Records and Network Records (otherwise known as Kool Kat records) helped introduce American and later Italian dance music to Britain. These labels also promoted UK dance music acts. By the end of the 1980s, UK DJs Jenö, Thomas, Markie and Garth moved to San Francisco, and called their group the Wicked Crew. The Wicked Crew's dance sound transmitted UK styles to the US, which helped to trigger the birth of the US west coast's rave scene.

# CHAPTER TWELVE

## ACID HOUSE

I n reality, Acid House had already started in Chicago in 1985. DJ Pierre and some friends pushed a button on their Roland 303 and found that that Acid sound was already in it. They produced a track called "Acid Trax" which, they allege, was stolen by Ron Hardy and delivered as "Ron Hardy's Acid Trax".

As Pierre once said,

---

"Phuture was me and two other guys, Spanky and Herbert J. We had this Roland 303, which was a bassline machine, and we were trying to figure out how to use it. When we switched it on, that acid sound was already in it and we liked the sound of it so we decided to add some drums and make a track with it. We gave it to Ron Hardy who started playing it straight away. In fact, the first time he played it, he played it four times in one night! The first time people were like, 'what the fuck is it?' but by the fourth they loved it. Then I started to hear that Ron was playing some new thing they were calling 'Ron Hardy's Acid Trax', and everybody thought it was something he'd made himself. Eventually we found out that it was our track so we called it 'Acid Trax'. I think we may have made it as early as 1985, but Ron was playing it for a long time before it came out."

---

There have been various explanations for the term 'Acid'. The most popular was that acid used to be put in the water at the Music Box. Pierre though, emphasises that Phuture was always anti-drugs, and cites a track about a cocaine nightmare, "Your only friend" that was on the same EP as "Acid Trax". "Acid Trax" came out in 1986 but did not prove to be successful outside Chicago. The first Acid track to make it to vinyl was called "I've Lost Control" which was made by Adonis and Marshall Jefferson.

# CHAPTER THIRTEEN

## LYRICAL THEMES

House lyrics contained positive, uplifting messages for all people, from every different walk of life but spoke especially to those who were considered to be outcasts, especially African-Americans and the gay subculture. As well, house music lyrics encouraged unity and called for people of all ethnic groups and backgrounds to come together. The house music dance scene was one of the most integrated and progressive spaces in the 1980s; gays, blacks, and other minority groups were able to dance together in a positive environment. Frankie Knuckles once said that the Warehouse club in Chicago was like "church for people who have fallen from grace". House record producer Marshall Jefferson compared it to "old-time religion in the way that people just get happy and screamin'". Deep house lyrics also contained messages calling for equality for the black community. However, not all house music songs had vocals, and in some cases, the vocals were wordless, as the most important element in house was the beat and rhythm. This contrasts sharply with pop music, which forefronts the vocal melody and the song lyrics.

## CHAPTER FOURTEEN

## A LOOK BACK AT THE 1970S

The 1970s was arguably the single decade of the 20th century when recorded music was most central to culture. There were, of course, fewer kinds of media competing for the average consumer's time —television meant just a handful of channels, video games were the size of refrigerators and could be found in arcades. As the used vinyl bins of the world are still telling us, records were the thing. Labels were flush with cash, sales of LPs and singles were brisk, and record stores were everywhere. Home stereos were a standard part of middle-class culture. Analog recording technology was at its zenith, FM radio was ascendant, and the AM dial still focused on music. The children of the baby boom were coming into their late twenties and thirties—young enough to still be serious music consumers, but old enough to have their own generation of children who were starting to buy music.

And then there was the music itself. Disco, an entire cultural movement fueled by a genre of music—with massive impact on fashion, film, TV and advertising—was utterly ubiquitous. Rock music emerged from the '60s as to go-to choice of white youth culture. Soul and funk were reaching new levels of artistry. Punk, the first serious backlash against the rock mainstream, came into its own. Records from Jamaica were making their way to the UK and, eventually, the U.S., changing sounds and urging a new kind of political consciousness. As culture moved in every direction at once, there were more great songs than anyone could count.

# CHAPTER FIFTEEN

## MARIANNE FAITHFULL

"There's no shame in being a muse—preening in silk robes on the couch, tousled hair parting to reveal full lips pouting around a cigarette, tossing off bon mots of aching elegance that nestle into the subconscious and reappear as pop hits."

If that's how Mick Jagger wanted to spend his days, more power to him. Marianne Faithfull was most famous in the '60s as the blonde, boho moll of the Rolling Stones frontman, whose career was twined to his and widely assumed dependent on his gifts: her version of the Stones' "As Tears Go By" was a hit in England; her near-fatal heroin overdose became "Wild Horses," and her literary interests begat "Sympathy for the Devil;" she co-wrote "Sister Morphine." But Jagger was also something of

Faithfull's muse, inspiring many entries in her prodigious Decca Records output of the late 1960s.

By the end of the 1970s, a decade in which she'd weathered drug abuse and homelessness (and long ended her high-profile love), Faithfull refused to be diminished for one more day. Broken English, her first rock record in 12 years, was the comeback triumph no one expected, not least in how gritty it was. The chilling title track is a prophetic merging of punk and dance, with lyrics that plumb the depths of her losses. "Could have come through anytime/Cold lonely, puritan," she intones harshly, gliding into a bloodless snarl that would make Johnny Rotten flinch. "What are you fighting for?/It's not my security." It's a terse, battle-scarred declaration of autonomy with hairpin melodic turns, early in its embrace of dance music's dark possibilities. "Broken English" is the portrait of a true survivor, starting a new era on her terms, alone.

# CHAPTER SIXTEEN

## PATRICE RUSHEN

Even as her sensibilities shifted from jazz to fusion to R&B and disco, Patrice Rushen focused on her keyboards while everything else swirled around them. On "Haven't You Heard," the piano is an anchor for the song. This can make it feel like an early skeleton of house music, which is appropriate—it was a touchstone of Larry Levan's sets at the Paradise Garage, and was eventually reborn as gospel house in Kirk Franklin's 2005 single "Looking for You."

"Haven't You Heard" is a formally perfect expression of disco. The best disco songs imply infinity in both their length and groove, and always feel as if they're attached to a black hole. "Haven't You Heard" enhances time until it feels like the glitter of a cityscape unfurling through a cab window. It manages this even as the lyric itself is private—

the literal text of a classified ad. "It only says 'I'm looking for the perfect guy,'" Rushen sings, searching for connection not through direct communication but with ambient speech. This kind of intimacy, personified by the whispery translucence of Rushen's voice, is just as easily exported to the dance floor.

# CHAPTER SEVENTEEN

## WAYLON JENNINGS

L ike the best outlaw country, "Are You Sure Hank Done It This Way?" looks backwards and forwards simultaneously, finding inspiration in the past even as it wonders what's around the next curve in the road. Jennings and his peers were traditionalists who bucked the very notion of tradition. All of them had been manhandled by the industry, but few bristled against the mainstream quite as strongly as Jennings, who found himself on a series of poorly planned tours that left him deep in debt to his label and addicted to amphetamines.

If this were just a song about all the "rhinestone suits and new shiny cars" that defined country music around the bicentennial, it would have been only a minor antagonism. But outlaw country rarely gets credit for its humor or its self-deprecation, and what lends the song its gravity, aside from the world-weariness of Waylon's vocals, is his sly assessment of his own place in the industry. Despite the hits he'd been notching for a decade, he was still just another road warrior who idolized Hank Sr. but still saw him as an almost hilariously impossible standard against which to measure himself or anybody else.

# CHAPTER EIGHTEEN

## ART ENSEMBLE OF CHICAGO

A healthy portion of Chicago's musical avant-garde decamped for France in 1969, but the group that made the biggest splash in Paris was the Art Ensemble of Chicago. The band's exuberant stage show reinforced its members' organizing slogan—"Great Black Music: Ancient to the Future"—with bassist Malachi Favors often dressed like an Egyptian shaman and saxophonist Roscoe Mitchell donning the garb of a contemporary urbanite. Over the course of a dozen-plus records cut in the 1970s, the band's sound made good on the malleability suggested by this varied public image, as they created delicate improvisations and noise blowouts alike.

On "Théme de Yoyo," the opening song on a soundtrack to a now-forgotten film, the Art Ensemble's rhythm section offers up a funk groove. When the group's notoriously wild horn players enter, they begin by playing things pretty straight—only reaching for avant-garde theatrics in brief pauses of the swinging, mod theme. Guest vocalist Fontella Bass—the wife of Art Ensemble trumpeter Lester Bowie—contributes soulful phrasings that sound downright commercial until you focus on the absurdist lyrics ("Your fanny's like two sperm whales floating down the Seine"). No matter how out there each instrumentalist ventures, every feature spot contains references to the track's pop-song foundation. As a piece of free-jazz funk that predates Ornette Coleman's Prime Time band, "Théme de Yoyo" is an early reflection of the benefits the Art Ensemble reaped from their refusal to be tied to a single genre.

# CHAPTER NINETEEN

## JORGE BEN

"T aj Mahal" is ostensibly about the famous tomb in Agra, India. The building was created by the Mughal emperor Shah Jahan, as a tribute to his fourth wife, Mumtaz Mahal, after her death during the birth of the couple's 14th child. "Foi a mais linda historia de amor," sings the Brazilian singer Ben: "It was the most pretty story of love." The couple's romance must have been strong stuff: the tomb was commissioned the year after her death, in 1632, and wasn't finished until 1653, at a cost of approximately $827 million in today's dollars.

Ben's original version of the song, recorded for his 1972 album Ben, is a subdued gem. But the version recorded for his massive 1976 crossover album Africa Brasil exudes joy, sparks flying from every exuberant note. The record would end up getting Rod Stewart—whose "Do Ya Think

I'm Sexy?" bore a strong resemblance—sued. It's not diffi-cult, though, to see what Stewart saw in its jubilant DNA (unconsciously, according to his autobiography). "Taj Mahal" captures an unselfconscious excitement, a purity of a deeply familiar feeling, yet projects it at a scale that can cross decades centuries.

## CHAPTER TWENTY

## LEE PERRY & THE FULL EXPERIENCES

This track is really three '70s reggae classics in one: Max Romeo's "Chase the Devil," Prince Jazzbo's "Croaking Lizard," and Lee Perry's mix of both with his own vocals. All this and more gets tossed in the pot in the nearly seven-minute-long "Disco Devil."

"Disco" doesn't reference the flashy dance genre of the same name but rather the concept of the "discomix," a 12" vinyl format that contains a vocal song seamlessly followed by a dub remix or a deejay version (meaning a rapped performance over the rhythm track). Perry essentially released a dub version of the Romeo and Jazzbo tracks, then followed it with a dub of the dub. It's a particularly effective example of Perry's innovative, eccentric production style that transforms the studio into an instrument itself. The approach to "Disco Devil" demonstrates the many ways he was able to pull pieces of a song apart and put them back together, add snippets of lyrics and sounds, and shape deep bass and rippling guitar to glide as if underwater.

## CHAPTER TWENTY-ONE

## FRANKIE KNUCKLES & JAMIE PRINCIPLE, "YOUR LOVE"

Frankie Knuckles was the undisputed godfather of house music and its ambassador to the world. Knuckles cut his teeth in New York before moving to Chicago to run the Warehouse, where his elegant, tasteful take on house influenced several generations of future producers, DJs and dancers. He's put out countless 12-inches and remixes, toured the world many times over, and had a street in Chicago named after him. Sadly, he passed away last year at the age of 59. This masterpiece is probably his best known track, and rightfully so.

# CHAPTER TWENTY-TWO

## JESSE SAUNDERS, "ON AND ON"

On and On" is widely considered to be the first proper house record. It starts with screams and maniacal laughter, then oozes along, with a healthy dose of reverb and twinkly synths as a top line, never quite fully banging into a typical hands-in-the-air crescendo the way we've come to expect from a house record. But it's evidence that house has never been singular. It can be many things. "On and On" is a gauzy 4 a.m. jam to bridge night into morning.

# CHAPTER TWENTY-THREE

## MARSHALL JEFFERSON, "MOVE YOUR BODY"

The stomping live piano intro is cited as the first time live pianos were utilized in house music, a trend that would rage on into the '90s and beyond. Marshall Jefferson is 55 years old and still going strong on the club and festival circuit.

## CHAPTER TWENTY-FOUR

### EARLY "JACKMASTER" FUNK FEAT. DARRYL PANDY "LOVE CAN'T TURN AROUND"

This is part cover, part re-interpretation of the Isaac Hayes track "I Can't Turn Around," which was also covered by Steve "Silk" Hurley (Farley's roommate at the time). Darryl Pandy is an absolute beast on this track, and it was the first house single to break into the U.K. singles chart.

## CHAPTER TWENTY-FIVE

## THE HOUSE MASTER BOYZ & THE RUDE BOY OF HOUSE, "HOUSE NATION"

Another Farley "Jackmaster" Funk, credited to his alias, The House Master Boyz. "Hu-Hu-Hu-Hu-Hu-Hu-House Nation" is pretty much all you need to get sucked into a hypnotic, liminal space of dance floor bewilderment and enlightenment.

# CHAPTER TWENTY-SIX

## MR. FINGERS, "CAN YOU FEEL IT"

Fingers Inc. was a Chicago house supergroup, featuring Larry Heard, aka Mr. Fingers, Robert Owens, and Ron Wilson. In Can You Feel It?" — originally released as a Mr. Fingers B-side in 1986, re-released and credited to Fingers Inc. in 1988 — they made what might just be a perfect record. The preacher vocals, the alien bassline, the cracking drums. It would become a blueprint for deep house, its moodiness and melancholia trumping its hedonism. It has been copied, again and again and again, with varying degrees of success.

# CHAPTER TWENTY-SEVEN

## JOE SMOOTH, "PROMISED LAND"

On the other end of the tonal spectrum, Joe Smooth's "Promised Land" is an uplifting, spiritual anthem about rising above the horrible realities of inner city life in the Reagan years, but its themes are universal. Perfect for closing out any set and sending the punters home filled with euphoric warm fuzzies.

CHAPTER TWENTY-EIGHT

ADONIS, "NO WAY BACK"

"**N**o Way Back" wastes no time diving into its bouncy, wonky baseline. It's been called dystopian and fatalist. Adonis Smith also provided the deadpan vocals, which are simultaneously off-putting and body-jacking. The record was a huge commercial hit for Trax Records, Chicago's most visible house imprint, which originally released most of the tracks on this list.

# CHAPTER TWENTY-NINE

## RON HARDY, "SENSATION"

Hardy was the Chicago house scene's loose cannon. He played fast, aggressive and loud. His reel-to-reel edits inspired decades of DJs trying to recreate an edit they once heard at the Muzic Box, his stomping ground, which had a walloping sound system. He burned hard and bright, dying in 1992 at the age of 33 of a heroin overdose, according to Michaelangelo Matos' recent book on the history of dance music in the U.S., The Underground Is Massive. "Sensation" is one of the few records he made that was released in his lifetime.

# CHAPTER THIRTY

## A LOOK BACK AT THE EIGHTIES

The 1980s saw the emergence of dance music and new wave. As disco fell out of fashion in the decade's early years, genres such as post-disco, Italo disco, Euro disco and dance-pop became more popular. Rock music continued to enjoy a wide audience. Soft rock, glam metal, thrash metal, shred guitar characterized by heavy distortion, pinch harmonics and whammy bar abuse became very popular. Adult contemporary, quiet storm, and smooth jazz gained popularity. In the late 1980s, glam metal became the largest, most commercially successful brand of music in the United States and worldwide.

The 1980s are commonly remembered for an increase in the use of digital recording, associated with the usage of synthesisers, with synth-pop music and other electronic genres featuring non-traditional instruments increasing in popularity. Also during this decade, several major electronic genres were developed, including electro, techno, house, freestyle and Eurodance, rising in prominence during the 1990s and beyond. Throughout the decade, R&B, hip hop and urban genres were becoming commonplace, particularly in the inner-city areas of large, metropolitan cities; rap was especially successful in the latter part of the decade, with the advent of the golden age of hip hop. These urban genres—particularly rap and hip hop—would continue their rise in popularity through the 1990s and 2000s.

The 1980s saw the reinvention of Michael Jackson, the superstardom of Prince, and the emergence of Madonna and Whitney Houston, —who were all the among most successful musicians during this time. Their videos became a permanent fixture on MTV and gained a worldwide mass audience. Michael Jackson was the first African American artist to have his music video aired on MTV in heavy rotation, Donna Summer was the first African American female artist to do the same. Michael Jackson's Thriller album from 1982 is the best-selling album of all time; it is cited as selling as many as 110 million copies worldwide.

Being the biggest selling album of that decade, it sold 20 million albums in the US and an additional 5 million worldwide. He was the one biggest star of the 1980s. Madonna was the most successful female artist of the decade. Her third studio album, True Blue, became the best-selling female album of the 1980s. Other Madonna albums from the decade include Like a Virgin which became one of the best selling albums of all-time and Like a Prayer, which was called "as close to art as pop music gets" by Rolling Stone. Madonna made music videos a marketing tool and was among the first to make them an art form. Many of her songs topped the Charts around the world, such as: "Like a Virgin", "Papa Don't Preach", "La Isla Bonita" and "Like a Prayer". After her Like a Prayer album release in 1989, Madonna was named artist of the decade by a number of magazines and awards.

Whitney Houston became one of the best selling female artist of the decade selling 15 millions albums in the US, behind Madonna and Barbra Streisand. Her eponymous debut studio album Whitney Houston became the best-selling debut album by a female artist, and her sophomore album became the first by a female debut at no. 1 in the history of Billboard 200 and she was the first and the only artist to chart seven consecutive number-one songs on the Billboard 100. By 1980, the prominent disco genre, largely dependent on orchestras, had become heavily unfavoured, replaced by a lighter synthpop production, which subsequently fuelled dance music. In the latter half of the 1980s, teen pop experienced its first wave, with bands and artists including Exposé, Debbie Gibson, Tiffany, New Edition, Stacey Q, The Bangles, New Kids on the Block, Madonna, George Michael, Laura Branigan, Boy George and others becoming teen idols.

Prominent American urban pop acts of the 1980s include Tina Turner, Lionel Richie, Michael Jackson, Donna Summer, Whitney Houston and Diana Ross. African American artists like Lionel Richie and Prince went on to become some of the decade's biggest pop stars. Their commercial albums included 1999, Purple Rain, and Sign "O" the Times by Prince and Lionel Richie, Can't Slow Down and Dancing on the Ceiling by Richie. Prince was the decade's most prolific artist, not just by virtue of being the top charting artist in the US and worldwide. He was responsible for artists such as Vanity 6, for whom he wrote the dance chart topping "Nasty Girl". Morris Day and the Time, he wrote the top 20 "Jungle Love" for. Sheila E., he wrote the top 10 song "The Glamorous Life", and number 11 "A Love Bizarre" with, as well as Wendy & Lisa and Apollonia 6. He wrote "I Feel for You" for Chaka Khan number 3 pop hit, number 1 on the R & B chart; which won him a Grammy for best R & B song. "Sugar Walls" for Sheena Easton, as well as doing a duet The Look, both top 10 hits; and "Manic Monday" #2 pop hit, for the Bangles. Artists that covered his music included Tom Jones, who brought his version of the song "Kiss", into the top 40 for the second time in the decade. Melissa Morgan brought her cover of "Do Me Baby" to the top of the R & B charts in 1986. Other notable artists that covered Prince, during the 1980s were The Pointer Sisters and Cyndi Lauper. He also won an Academy Award for the song "Purple Rain". In 1989, Irish singer Sinead O'Connor would record a cover of "Nothing Compares 2 U", which would become the biggest song of the year worldwide, in the new decade to follow.

House music already important in the 1980s dance club scene, eventually house penetrated the UK pop charts. London DJ "Evil" Eddie Richards spun at dance parties as resident at the Clink Street club. Richards' approach to house focuses on the deep basslines. Nicknamed the UK's "Godfather of House", he and Clink co-residents Kid Batchelor and Mr. C played a key role in early UK house. House first charted in the UK in Wolverhampton following on from the success of the Northern Soul scene. The record generally credited as the first house hit in the UK was Farley "Jackmaster" Funk's "Love Can't Turn Around", which reached #10 in the UK singles chart in September 1986. The acid house record "The Only Way Is Up" by Yazz was the second best-selling British single of 1988.

In January 1987, Chicago DJ/artist Steve "Silk" Hurley's "Jack Your Body" reached number one in the UK, showing it was possible for house music to achieve crossover success in the pop charts. The same month also saw Raze enter the top 20 with "Jack the Groove", and several further house hits reached the top ten that year. Stock Aitken Waterman (SAW) expensively-produced productions for Mel and Kim, including the number-one hit "Respectable", added elements of house to their previous Europop sound. SAW session group Mirage scored top-ten hits with "Jack Mix II" and "Jack Mix IV", medleys of previous electro and Europop hits rearranged in a house music style. Key labels in the rise of house music in the UK included:

1. Jack Trax, which specialized in licensing US club hits for the British market and released an influential series of compilation albums.
2. Rhythm King, which was set up as a hip hop label but also issued house record In March 1987, the UK tour of influential US DJs such as Knuckles, Jefferson, Fingers Inc. (Heard) and Adonis, on the DJ International Tour boosted house's popularity in the UK. Following the number-one success of MARRS' "Pump Up The Volume" in October, in 1987 to 1989, UK acts such as The Beatmasters, Krush, Coldcut, Yazz, Bomb The Bass, S-Express, and Italy's Black Box opened the doors to house music success on the UK charts. Early British house music quickly set itself apart from the original Chicago house sound. Many of the early hits were based on sample montage, and unlike the US soulful vocals, in UK house, rap was often used for vocals (far more than in the US), and humor and wit was an important element.

# CHAPTER THIRTY-ONE

## IBIZA

House was also being developed by DJs and record producers in the booming dance club scene in Ibiza. While no house artists or labels came from this tiny island at the time, mixing experiments and innovations done by Ibiza DJs helped to influence the house style. By the mid-1980s a distinct Balearic mix of house was discernible. Several influential clubs in Ibiza, such as Amnesia, with DJ Alfredo at the decks, were playing a mix of rock, pop, disco and house. These clubs, fuelled by their distinctive sound and copious consumption of the club drug Ecstasy, began to influence the British scene. By late 1987, DJs such as Trevor Fung, Paul Oakenfold and Danny Rampling were bringing the Ibiza sound to key UK clubs such as the Haçienda in

Manchester. Ibiza influences also spread to DJs working London clubs such as Shoom in Southwark, Heaven, Future and Spectrum.

In the U.S., house music developed into more sophisticated sound, moving beyond the rudimentary drum machine loops and short samples that had characterized early US house. In Chicago, Marshall Jefferson formed the house group Ten City with Byron Burke, Byron Stingily & Herb Lawson (from "Intensity"). New York City–based performers such as Mateo & Matos and Blaze had slickly produced disco-infused house tracks. In Detroit a proto-techno music sound began to emerge with the DJ record-ings and mixes of Juan Atkins, Derrick May and Kevin Saunderson.

Atkins, a former member of Cybotron, released "No UFOs" as Model 500 in 1985, which became a regional hit. Atkins follow this by dozens of tracks on Transmat, Metroplex and Fragile. One of the most unusual songs was "Strings of Life" by Derrick May (under the name Rhythim Is Rhythim), a darker, more intellectual strain of house. "Techno-Scratch" was released by the Knights Of The Turntable in 1984 which had a similar techno sound to Cybotron. The manager of the Factory nightclub and co-owner of the Haçienda, Tony Wilson, also promoted acid house culture on his weekly TV show. The UK midlands also embraced the late 1980s house scene with illegal parties and raves and more legal dance clubs such as The Hummingbird.

# CHAPTER THIRTY-TWO

## HOUSE EIGHTIES & NINETIES AND THE WORLD

In America, the house scene had still not progressed beyond a small number of clubs in Chicago, Detroit, Newark and New York City. Newark-area DJ Tony Humphries was influenced the sounds of disco pioneer David Mancuso, the host of the disco-era's underground gay subculture loft parties. Humphries played his mixes in Newark NJ's Club Zanzibar, where he developed his signature "Jersey Sound", which mixed a soulful element with a rawer edge. Many independent Chicago-based record labels were also getting their artists on the dance charts. Detroit DJ Terrence Parker uses his advanced turntablism skills and his focus on precision to blend hip hop music DJing styles, such as rhythmic scratching, in his house mixes. Fellow Detroit spinner DJ Minx is a notable woman house DJ. Her records on her Women on Wax label blend Parker-influenced turntablism precision with a funky style.

In the UK, any house song released by a Chicago-based label was routinely considered a "must-play" at UK house music clubs. Paradise Garage in New York City was still a top club in the house era, just as it had been during the disco age. The emergence of Todd Terry, a pioneer of the genre, demonstrated the continuum from the underground disco approach which moved to a new house sound. Terry's cover of Class Action's "Weekend" (mixed by Larry Levan) shows how Terry drew on newer hip-hop influences, such as the quicker sampling and the more rugged basslines.

In the late 1980s, Nu Groove Records launched and nurtured the careers of Rheji Burrell & Rhano Burrell, collectively known as Burrell (after a brief stay on Virgin America via Timmy Regisford and Frank Mendez). Nu Groove also had a stable of other NYC underground scene DJs. The Burrell's created the "New York Underground" sound of house, and they did 30+ releases on this label featuring this sound. In the 2010s, Nu Groove Record releases like the Burrells' enjoy a cult status among "crate diggers" and DJs. Mint-condition vinyl records by the Burrells from the 1980s can fetch high prices.

By the late 1980s, house DJing and production had

moved to the US's west coast, particularly to San Francisco, Oakland, Los Angeles, Fresno, San Diego and Seattle. Los Angeles saw am explosion of underground raves, where DJs mixed dance tracks. L.A. DJs Marques Wyatt and Billy Long spun at Jewel's Catch One. In 1989, the L.A.-based, former EBN-OZN singer/rapper Robert Ozn started indie house label One Voice Records. Ozn released the Mike "Hitman" Wilson remix of Dada Nada's "Haunted House", which garnered club and mix show radio play in Chicago, Detroit and New York as well as in the U.K. and France. The record went up to number five on the Billboard Club Chart, marking it as the first house record by a white (Caucasian) artist to chart in the U.S. Dada Nada, the moniker for Ozn's solo act, did his first releases in 1990, using a jazz-based Deep House style. The Frankie Knuckles and David Morales remix of Dada Nada's "Deep Love" (One Voice Records in the US, Polydor in the UK), featuring Ozn's lush, crooning vocals and jazzy improvisational solos by muted trumpet, underscored Deep House's progression into a genre that integrated jazz and pop songwriting and song forms (unlike acid house and techno).

In the early 1990s, house music became more popular in the US. Pop singer Madonna's house-infused 1990 single "Vogue" became an international hit single and topped the US charts. The single is credited as helping to bring house music to the US mainstream. The gospel/R&B-influenced "Time Passes On" in 1993 (Strictly Rhythm), then later, U.S.

hit which received radio play was the single "Time for the Perculator" by Cajmere, which became the prototype for the emerging ghetto house subgenre. Cajmere started the Cajual and Relief labels (amongst others). By the early 1990s, artists of note included Cajmere (under that name as well as Green Velvet and as producer for Dajae), DJ Sneak, and Glenn Underground. The 1990s saw new Chicago house artists emerge, such as DJ Funk, who operates a Chicago house record label called Dance Mania. Ghetto house and acid house were other house music styles that started in Chicago.

In Britain, further experiments in the genre boosted its appeal. House and rave clubs such as Lakota and Cream emerged across Britain, hosting house and dance scene events. The 'chilling out' concept developed in Britain with ambient house albums such as The KLF's Chill Out and Analogue Bubblebath by Aphex Twin. The Godskitchen superclub brand also began in the midst of the early 90's rave scene. After initially hosting small nights in Cambridge and Northampton, the associated events scaled up in Milton Keynes, Birmingham and Leeds. A new indie dance scene also emerged in the 90's. In New York, bands such as Deee-Lite furthered house's international influence. Two distinctive tracks from this era were the Orb's "Little Fluffy Clouds" (with a distinctive vocal sample from Rickie Lee Jones) and the Happy Mondays' "Wrote for Luck" ("WFL") which was transformed into a dance hit by Vince Clarke.

In England, one of the few licensed venues was The Eclipse, which attracted people from up and down the country as it was open until the early hours. Due to the lack of licensed, legal dance event venues, house music promoters began organising illegal events in unused warehouses, aeroplane hangars and in the countryside. The Criminal Justice and Public Order Act 1994 was a government attempt to ban large rave dance events featuring music with "repetitive beats", due to law enforcement allegations that these events were associated with illegal club drugs. There were a number of "Kill the Bill" demonstrations by rave and electronic dance music fans. The Spiral Tribe dance event at Castle Morten was the last of these illegal raves, as the bill, which became law, in November 1994, made unauthorised house music dance events illegal in the UK. Despite the new law, the music continued to grow and change, as typified by Left-field with "Release the Pressure", which introduced dub and reggae into the house sound. Leftfield's prior releases, such as "Not Forgotten" released in 1990 on Shef-field's Outer Rhythm records used a more typical sound.

A new generation of clubs such as Liverpool's Cream and the Ministry of Sound were opened to provide a venue for more commercial house sounds. Major record companies began to open "superclubs" promoting their own groups and acts. These superclubs entered into sponsorship deals initially with fast food, soft drink, and clothing companies. Flyers in clubs in Ibiza often sported many corporate logos from sponsors. A new subgenre, Chicago hard house, was developed by DJs such as Bad Boy Bill, DJ Lynnwood, and DJ Irene, Richard "Humpty" Vission, mixing elements of Chicago house, funky house and hard house. Additionally, producers such as George Centeno, Darren Ramirez, and Martin O. Cairo developed the Los Angeles Hard House sound. Similar to gabber or hardcore techno from the Netherlands, this was associated with the "rebel", underground club subculture of the time. These three producers introduced new production approaches and sounds in late 20th century became more prominent and widely used during first decade of the 21st century.

Towards the end of the 1990s and into the 2000s (decade), French DJ/producers such as Daft Punk, Stardust, Cassius, St. Germain and DJ Falcon began producing a new sound in Paris' club scene. Together, they laid the ground-work for what would be known as the French house movement. They combined the harder-edged-yet-soulful philosophy of Chicago house with the melodies of obscure funk records. As well, by using state-of-the-art digital production techniques blended with the retro sound of old-school analog synthesizers, they created a new sound and style which influenced house music around the world.

## CHAPTER THIRTY-THREE

## HOUSE ALBUMS OF THE NINETIES

House music has grown wide and tall in the three decades since it first took root in the after-hours clubs of Chicago. These days it is a global phenomenon with its own industry and countless distinct sub-cultures, sounds, and social movements branching off from the source. It's so big that when one person says they're "into house music," you can't exactly be sure what they're referring to—is it the slick, hypnotic house of Ibiza? The piano-heavy diva house of '90s New York? The more restrained minimal house you're likely to hear in Berlin?

Even at the turn of the '90s—only five or six years after the term "house music" had been uttered for the first time—the movement had reached the far corners of Europe and the Americas. The Brits in particular ran with the new records from Chicago, Detroit, and New York and added their own experimental edge to the mix, giving birth to the beginnings of rave culture. In the U.S., house music had already climbed the pop charts by the late '80s, and underground producers were signing major label contracts. There were formidable domestic movements in Belgium, France, Italy, Japan, and South Africa, each with their own sound and style.

And while the decade's great producers are known more for successful club singles and mixtapes than for their long-players, a few memorable albums emerged from those early years. Below you can dig into a wide-reaching selection of LPs that illustrate the many forms that house music took as it began to mature into the music we know today.

## 808 State, Utd. State 90

This pop crossover from the dawn of the decade is about as '90s as it gets. It's got that funky De La Soul font with outrageous primary color combos and some of the era's most eccentric B-boy attire. With a trio formed by Japanese producer Towa Tei, Ukrainian expat DJ Dmitry, and American front-woman Lady Miss Kier, it's about as multicultural as an early Benetton ad. World Clique is the debut record from Deee-lite, who you may remember from the ultimate wedding party request "Groove Is in the Heart." The group formed in 1986 in Williamsburg, Brooklyn, and pretty much defined the campy, hip-house sound of Top 40 radio in New York at the time.

Younger fans may know Armand Van Helden as one half of Duck Sauce, the contemporary duo behind silly big-room hits like "Barbra Streisand." But Armand was also one of the star artists associated with New York imprint Strictly Rhythm, arguably the most important house label of the '90s. While many of his productions from the late '90s and early 'oos tended to touch on the more UK-centric breakbeat sound championed by acts like Fatboy Slim, tracks like "Witch Doktor" are essential parts of New York house history. The Funk Phenomena is his debut album, which includes many of the tracks that first catapulted him to international acclaim.

## Mr. Fingers, Introduction

Mr. Fingers is Larry Heard, a totemic figure in the history of Chicago house music. His 1986 master work "Can You Feel It?"—produced alongside Robert Owens and Robert Wilson as Fingers Inc.—endures today as one of the genre's most iconic tracks, and has been remixed and reworked by countless producers who came after.

Throughout various interviews, Heard has characterized himself as an instrumentalist who prefers the more organic songwriting process to computer-based composition, and his 1992 album testifies to that. While much of it is built on top of drum machines and synths, it often sounds more like fully formed R&B or soul than the stripped-back club tracks many of his contemporaries were producing at the time.

## Black Box, Dreamland

The double platinum-selling debut album from the Italian group Black Box played a huge role in bringing house music to pop radio the world over. It wasn't without its share of controversy, however. First, the group came under fire for their heavy—and unlicensed, uncredited—sampling of pop star Loleatta Holloway on their breakout single, "Ride on Time." Then, their label was forced to pay a large settlement to their hired vocalist, the American R&B singer Martha Wash, who Black Box failed to credit on any of the six songs she recorded with them. To add insult to injury, the group then hired a tall, skinny model to lip-sync in the music video for their album's second single—rather than giving camera time to the more heavy-set Wash. Despite the deeply shady business dealings, Dreamland remains one of the most iconic albums of the '90s, even for non-house heads.

## Danny Tenaglia, Hard & Soul

Danny Tenaglia never enjoyed the pop success of contemporaries like Armand Van Helden or Deee-lite, but to this day he remains one of the seminal figures in New York house music. The prolific DJ and producer began his career in Brooklyn, DJing at roller discos in the late '70s and early '80s and later became a resident at legendary downtown dance spots like Twilo, Tunnel, and Vinyl. Hard & Soul is his debut full-length, and it helped define the sound of "tribal house" (as it was called at the time), a percussion-heavy style that often veered into darker, more ominous territory than the feel-good tracks coming out at the time. You can still catch Tenaglia playing all-night sets at spots like Output in Brooklyn or Space in Ibiza.

## Masters at Work

"Little" Louie Vega and Kenny "Dope" Gonzalez are two of the most prolific producers in the history of house music. Together as Masters at Work, they helped define the funky, Latin-flavored sound of the New York club scene in particular and can still be found controlling the decks at top dance spots downtown. This 1993 album provides a vivid illustration of how hip-hop, house, and reggae once mingled on the streets of NYC, with an opening track that features Jamaican dancehall emcee Screechie Dan.

## Theo Parrish, First Floor

If you prefer your grooves rough around the edges, Theo Parrish's 1998 debut album is the one for you. First Floor saw the Chicago-born, Detroit-based producer re-writing all the rules with his unkempt and unfussy approach to deep, soulful house. Much like Moodymann, Parrish weaves a vibrant tapestry of gospel and soul sound bytes —though his stuttering loops, damaged samples, and general lack of respect for musical conventions set him apart from the rest of the pack. His famously adventurous DJ sets—which extend up to eight hours—touch on a broad range of genres across four or five decades, and have given him a reputation as one of the great record diggers of our time.

## Daft Punk, Homework

It's a harrowing thought that there's a generation of tweens who have only ever heard Daft Punk's comeback album, Random Access Memories. In case you were in Huggies the first time around, let's be clear that the duo's 1997 album is the crowning jewel of French electronic music. While acts like Fatboy Slim were conquering the electronic charts with a juiced-up, rave-ready breakbeat sound, Thomas

Bangalter and Guy-Manuel de Homem-Christo were taking a different tact by bringing disco and funk to the fore. Their singular style turned a generation of teenagers in rock bands onto the joys of drum machines, samplers, and synthesizers, and changed the face of pop culture in the process.

## CHAPTER THIRTY-FOUR

## IT'S ALL ABOUT THE DEEP HOUSE

Way back in the mid-1980s, when the disco gurus appeared over the Chicago skyline and proclaimed, "Let there be house," his acolytes responded, "And let it be deep." And it was good.

Slower, moodier, and more sensual than most other club-music forms — heir to disco at its most mirrorball-blissful — deep house has survived for nearly three decades, staying mostly out of the spotlight, consigned to warm-up sets and after-hours reveries. But lately, it has bubbled back to the surface.

This month, the soulful sound scored a No. 1 hit on the U.K. pop charts with Storm Queen's "Look Right Through," a

'90s-flavored song by Metro Area's Morgan Geist and busker extraordinaire Damon C. Scott that was first released on Geist's Environ label in 2010. It was a more recent remix from '90s deep-house mainstay MK (Marc Kinchen), and a summer's worth of heavy club play, that finally pushed it to the top slot, on the back of MK's recent success with remixes for Lana Del Rey, Sky Ferreira, and Disclosure.

"Look Right Through" wasn't a fluke. Duke Dumont's "Need U (100%)," another U.K. No. 1, has logged more than 17 million plays on YouTube; its plunging bass line and sub-aquatic keyboard stabs are direct descendants of Kerri Chandler's deep-diving take on New Jersey garage. Disclosure, the year's biggest dance-pop crossover success story, draw heavily from the deep-house playbook in their lanky grooves and woozy atmospheres. Behind them, there's a veritable groundswell of deep-house revivalists: Jamie Jones, Maya Jane Coles, Breach, Dixon and the Innervisions crew, Axel Boman, Hot Since 82 — even Bloc Party's Kele Okereke has plunged into the full-fathom sound.

In fact, 21 of Beatport's current Top 100 tracks are tagged as deep house. That doesn't make it the most popular genre on the site, but after big-room electro house, it's tied for second place with progressive house, and boasts a stronger chart presence than tech house (14 tracks), house (12), indie dance (four), and techno and trance (two apiece).

Remember dubstep? That particular wub-genre doesn't have a single song in the Top 100.

A few years ago, that would have been unthinkable; deep house's moody pulses were drowned out in a cacophony of lasers and jackhammers and drops. But deep house's deliberately low profile is beginning to bear out the old meek-will-inherit-the-earth maxim.

Why now? In part, it's a reaction to the ubiquity of EDM at its most garish and bottle-serviced. Warm, moody, some-times hesitant, and often melancholic, deep house is the antithesis of mainstream EDM's harder/faster/stronger ethos, that capitalist ego-topia fueled by cheap presets and dodgy Molly, hell-bent on success. Deep house is contradictory, wracked with doubt, so full of blue notes it bleeds indigo. It's pro-sadness on the dance floor; pro-pathos in the mix.

Ironically, the success of deep house as an alternative to big-tent EDM has helped it creep towards the mainstream. Pete Tong's "Essential New Tune" selections increasingly lean toward deep house breakout stars like Jamie Jones and Richy Ahmet, while the rest of his show favors crossover cornballs like Afrojack and Avicii; even trance grandmaster Tiësto now has a weekly deep house radio show on Sirius XM.

We'll be the first to admit that some of the attention has been misplaced. A lot of what gets flogged as deep house right now isn't really worthy of the name; it's mid-tempo, pop-dance fare with a 2-step twist, or it's snoozy, monotone background music tailor-made for SEO plays on YouTube channels emblazoned with soft-lit hipster cheesecake. In fact, "deep house" itself is a retrospective term; in their heyday, many of the first songs in the canon were simply considered "house," full stop. It was only later that a style assembled itself around the template those originators had set.

So what classifies as deep house today? Some basic guidelines: The four-to-the-floor pulse is imbued with a suggestive bit of shuffle and swing, with accents on the two and four. The grooves are more restrained than techno's, leaning back rather than barreling forward. The tempo generally runs between 118 and 125 beats per minute, although there are many outliers. More than anything, deep house is rich in harmony and atmosphere, buoyant as a jellyfish, bursting with lush textures and phosphorescent tones. Taking the definition of deep house at its most elastic, we've selected 40 songs that trace its evolution across 27 years, one inky chord at a time.

House Music was the first direct descendant of Disco. It's said that "House was born from the ashes of Disco," covered further down about 'Disco Demolition Night.' Disco emerged in the early 70s as an underground movement born out of the urban culture in New York City. Predominantly African American and Latino communities popularized underground clubs and accelerated dance music culture.

House Music is a genre of dance music that has spread like a wildfire across the world. It has been keeping people dancing for well over 20 years and has become a lifestyle many have come to love and appreciate. Deriving from Disco, House Music has evolved into many sub-genres that have gained mass appeal and will continue to grow exponentially.

Club DJs began exploring mixing and beatmatching records, applying editing techniques, playing narrative DJ sets, and experimenting with innovative ways to overcome the limitations of the DJ equipment in those times. Many of these DJs helped merge the roles of DJ, composer, producer, and remixer by creating and playing their own edits of their favorite songs on reel-to-reel tape. Give up some love for House and keep the bass pumpin'.

# ABOUT THE AUTHOR

Eric Reese is an African American author, writer and blogger who had interest in writing since grade school (daily morning journals) but got caught up in the street life as he became older. After years of traveling throughout the world and meeting people of all walks of life, he finally found time to began writing down his experiences often using realistic situations in fictional works. You will find many of his stories in urban life, human trafficking, and thrillers based on probable cause.

---

**Lastly, kindly review this book on every book and audiobook platform possible. It's a once-in-a-lifetime request that will help spread House Music history .**

---

Made in United States
North Haven, CT
18 February 2025

66008433R10055